Leadership Skills

User Manual

Christopher G. Yorke, M.Ed.

Leadership Skills
User Manual

By Christopher G. Yorke, M. Ed.

Published by:

Mason Creek Publishing
35111 NE 94th Ave.
La Center, WA 98629
(360) 263-5780
cyorke57@gmail.com

Copyright 2018 by Mason Creek Publishing

ISBN 978-1984929426
Printed in the United States of America
Library of Congress CIP Data pending

Table of Contents

What is Leadership?

Review Questions

1. What is meant by the term "leadership?"
   A cluster of skills that contribute to your ability to work with other people in a productive manner.

2. List some things you need to be able to do in order to be a leader.
   Influence, motivate, inspire, be responsible, work hard, set goals, serve community, set positive example.

3. What are personal leadership/soft skills?
   Skills that make it possible for a person to interact positively with individuals and groups.

4. What are technical or hard skills?
   Skills needed to do a job.

5. Think of a situation in your life in which leadership skills would be useful. List the leadership skills you feel would be useful to you. This could be in your job, school, church, or even at home.

   Example Answers

   Restaurant Manager
   Communication
   Set a positive example
   Work hard
   Meeting management skills
   Speaking skills

The Skills Employers Want

Job Survey

Instructions:

Choose a job you are interested in.

Research the job and list the technical skills and the leadership skills required.

<u>Example Answers:</u>

Job Title: *Fireman*

Technical Skills:

Drive truck
Operate equipment
First Aid
Fight fires

Leadership Skills:

Communication
Sensitivity
Dedication
Trustworthy
Good work ethic
Follow through

Identifying Leadership Traits

Application

Instructions:

Think of someone you would classify as a good leader -- could be someone you know, have met, read about, or seen on television or in a movie. List the leadership traits displayed by that person. Use the list of leadership traits on page 9 as a guide. Add any traits you can think of that are not on the list.

Example Answers:

Name of Leader: *Mark Zuckerberg (Facebook CEO)*

Leadership Traits:

Original
Follow through
Initiative
Persistence
Desire to excel
Oral communication
Socially adaptable
Positive work ethic
Teamwork skills
Self confidence

Leadership Styles

Review Questions

Suggestion: Allow students to use the internet when identifying example leaders for this assignment.

1. Define laissez-faire leadership.
    Hands-off, delegative. Leader does not attempt to influence members. Gives most tasks to group members.

2. Write down someone you would characterize as a laissez-faire leader.
    Herbert Hoover, Warren Buffet, Queen Victoria.

3. Define autocratic leadership.
    Power centered. Group members are allowed little or no voice in decision making.

4. Write down someone you would characterize as an autocratic leader.
    Adolf Hitler, Napoleon Bonaparte, Genghis Khan.

5. Define participative leadership.
    Democratic. Shared authority and decision making.

6. Write down someone you would characterize as a participative leader.
    George Washington, Abraham Lincoln, Thomas Jefferson.

7. Define transformational leadership.
    Create vision of the future for the members. Frequent communication with members.

8. Write down someone you would characterize as a transformational leader.
    John Deere, Henry Ford, Walt Disney.

9. Define transactional leadership
    Structure and order are expected. Rewards and punishments are used to motivate members or employees. Managers and employers set goals.

10. Write down someone you would characterize as a transactional leader.
    Norman Schwarzkoph, Vince Lombardi, Bill Gates.

11. What do you think your leadership style is?
    Could be any one of the styles or a combination of styles.

12. Describe a situation where you would utilize a combination of different leadership styles.
    Working with a diverse group of people who respond to different leadership approaches.

Leadership Styles
Application

<u>Example Answers:</u>

1. Think of three people you know who are leaders. They could include class or club officers, advisors, committee chairpersons, business managers or political leaders. List each person by name, position, leadership style, and your rating of each person's effectiveness. (good, fair, poor).

Name	Position	Leadership Style	Effectiveness
Dan Smith	*Store Manager*	*Laissez-Faire*	*Fair*
Mr. Collins	*School Principal*	*Participative*	*Good*
Mary Black	*City Mayor*	*Autocratic*	*Poor*

2. Pick one of the leaders you have selected who is a good leader. Explain why you think this individual is an effective leader.

   Mr. Collins involves everyone, staff and students, in the decision making process at the school. People seem more positive and motivated under his style of leadership.

Goal Setting Worksheet

Name _Example_____ **Date**_____

Long-term Goal

Start a home construction company

Intermediate Goals

Get a job framing homes and start leaning to build houses
Earn a degree in construction management from the university

Short-term Goals

Find a any job to pay my bills

Apply to the university for fall semester

Order transcripts from my high school

Work out at the athletic club and stay in shape

What is a Group?

True or False Quiz

T or F

1. __T__ A group usually consists of three or more people.

2. __F__ People in groups have very little in common.

3. __F__ Groups and teams are very different.

4. __T__ Groups include people who have a common goal.

5. __F__ A club would not be considered to be a group.

6. __T__ There are formal and informal groups.

7. __F__ Examples of formal groups include a family and a group of friends.

8. __F__ Examples of informal groups include a sports team and a club.

9. __T__ Most organizations consist of a network of groups.

10. __T__ Understanding groups processes will help you participate in a group.

11. __F__ Individuals have little influence on a group.

12. __T__ The ability of the groups in an organization to interact will determine the success or failure of the organization.

Group Dynamics
Application

Example Answers:

1. List five different groups. Write the main goal of each group.

   Student Council - school activities
   Football Team - win games
   Teacher Staff - educate students
   Administrative Team - manage the school
   City Council - manage the city

2. Select one group from your list. What are the rules and expectations of the members of the group. What would happen if the members of the group did not abide by the rules and expectations of the group?

   Student Council

   Rules and Expectations of Members:

   Attend council meetings
   Be on time to meetings
   Help organize school activities
   Represent the school in a positive manner
   Set a positive example

   What would happen if members did not follow the rules and expectations?

   Meetings would not be productive
   Activities would not get organized

Group Norms

Application

Example Answers:

1. List a group you are involved with.
   ASB Student Leadership

2. List the group norms which apply to your group or organization.

   Things You Should Do:
   Help other students
   Listen to other's concerns
   Respect other ASB officers

   Things You Should Not Do:
   Should not insult others
   Should not use profanity

   Things You May Do:
   Offer suggestions
   Decide upon activities to get involved with

Roles of Group Members

Application

Example Answers:

Think of a group that you are a member of. The group could be at school, work, or at home.

Recreation committee at work.

What is your position in the group?

Member

List the specific roles you have in the group.

Decide on recreation activities for the year.

Organize activities.

Develop a budget.

Help conduct the activities.

Role Conflict

Application

Example Answers:

List all of the groups you are involved with. Remember that we are ALL involved with groups -- your family is a group.

ASB, Football team, Family, Jab at store.

In terms of the roles you play in the groups listed, are there any conflicts between the roles? Could there be conflict in the future. Write them down. What action can you take to reduce or manage these conflicts?

Potential Conflicts

ASB Meeting -- Football Games

Job - Family Responsibilities

Actions to Reduce Conflicts

Be in less groups.

Reduce job hours per week.

Use a calendar/schedule to manage time better.

Group Status
Application

Example Answers:

Think of one group you are involved with. List the group's management positions, such as officers, committee members, etc. Rate the positions (not the current people who hold the positions) according to your own evaluation of how much status each position has. For the status rating, use a scale of High, Medium, and Low.

Group Name _____ *FBLA Chapter* _____

Management Positions	**Status Rating**
President	*High*
Vice President	*High*
Secretary	*Medium*
Members	*Medium*
Advisor	*High*

Pick one of the people in your list that has attained a high level of status in the group. What kind of things did this person do to earn their level of status?

President - Responsible, polite, trustworthy, dedicated, hard working ...

Group Dynamics
Application

1. List five different groups. Write the main goal of each group.
   Student Council - school activities
   Football team - win football games
   Teacher staff - educate students
   Admin. team - manage the school
   City council - manage the city

2. Select one group from your list. What are the rules and expectations of the members of the group. What would happen if the members of the group did not abide by the rules and expectations of the group?

   Student Council

   Rules and Expectations of Members:
   Attend council meetings
   Be on time to meetings
   Help organize school activities
   Represent the school in a positive manner
   Set a positive example

   What would happen if members did not follow the rules and expectations?
   Meetings would not be productive
   Activities would not get organized

Teamwork
Application

<u>Example Answers:</u>

Answer the following questions about your organization and its various groups.

1. What characteristics can you list that indicate good group cohesiveness and teamwork between the people in your organization. This could be between members and officers, employees and managers, etc.

    Work together well

    Get things done

    Listen to each other

    Respect each other

    Loyal to the group

2. Are there any things that indicate a lack of cohesiveness or teamwork within the group?

    Sometimes members argue

    Sometimes members talk and interrupt others

    Sometimes members are late for meetings

3. What suggestions do you have that would help your organization increase group cohesiveness and teamwork?

    Learn to discuss matters without arguing

    Let each member speak without being interrupted

    Convince members to be on time to meetings

Teamwork and Group Cohesiveness
Small Group Application

Answers for this application will vary depending on the group.

List the names of the people in your group.

Work with a small group in your class or department. Discuss the concept of group cohesiveness and teamwork with your work group. Share the items you listed on the previous page about your organization's cohesiveness and teamwork.

Brainstorm five good ideas that could increase the cohesiveness and teamwork of the members of your organization. After your group agrees on five good items, list them on this page. Have someone write the items from each group on the board. Group similar items. The members of your organization should vote on the top 5 items they would like to see implemented.

Wait for three months or so after the items have been implemented. Hold another group meeting the determine if the items have made an impact on the cohesiveness and teamwork amongst the members of your organization. Make adjustments as necessary.

Group Pressure

Application

Example Answers:

Think of a group you are a member of. This could be at work, school, church, etc.

Day shift at my grocery store job

1. List the informal pressures you experience in the group.

   Pressure to dress like the other workers
   Pressure to hang out with the other workers after our shift

2. List the formal pressures you experience in the group.

   Pressure to be at work on time
   Pressure to greet customers a certain way
   Pressure to attend work meetings

3. What kinds of positive pressures could be used to motivate others to conform to the expectations of your group?

   Speaking to them positively
   Giving positive feedback
   Some type of reward system

Small Group Application
Observing Group Member Roles

Answers will vary depending on the group.

Work with a small group or committee. Discuss an important issue that is before your organization this year. For example, decide on the organization's theme for the year. As your group works on this task identify the different roles each member plays. Record your observations on the chart on page XX.

After your group has completed the task, discuss the roles that you observed. Share your results with the group.

During your small group discussion, observe the roles people play . What role did each person play? What actions did you observe about each person -- who played which role? Record your findings and discuss them with the members of your group.

Identifying Stressful Activities

Application

Example Answers:

Instructions:

List examples of stressful experiences that you have had in your life.
Keep this list nearby so you can use it for another exercise later in this chapter.

1. As a student

   Taking tests

2. As an officer, committee chairperson, or leader of an activity

   Leading meetings

3. As an employee

   Getting busy at the store

4. As a family member

   Helping sick parent

Effects of Stress

Application

Example Answers:

Instructions: Think of a recent situation or event in your life which you found to be stressful.

1. What was the event? Summarize it.

   Speaking in front of the entire school.

2. What specific things about this event are you able to identify as the cause of the stress?

   Being nervous.

   Fear of making mistakes.

3. What effects did this stress have on you? (headache, fatigue, irritability, etc.)

   Fatigue

   Irritable

   Sweating

4. Can you think of a situation where stress may have been helpful to you. Why was this a positive stress situation?

   Studying for a test.
   The stress of the upcoming test made me study harder.

Reducing Stress

Application

Example Answers:

1. List a stressful situation that you experienced during the past year.

   A coworker at the store got really mad at me.

2. How did you react in this stressful situation?

   I got angry and yelled at the other worker.

3. Could you have changed your reaction in order to reduce the stress level? Describe how.

   Yes. Could have stayed calm and talked the problem over.

4. If the stressful situation continued for several days, what methods did you use to help deal with the stress?

   Tried to think positively.

   Talked to the other worker about the disagreement and tried to get past it.

5. Are you aware of any other methods you could have used? Describe them.

Effective Listening Skills

True or False Quiz

1. ___T___   Sometimes listening can be more important than speaking.

2. ___T___   A person who is always talking and never listening is not really communicating.

3. ___T___   Daydreaming effectively closes down the possibility of retaining information.

4. ___F___   Developing a rebuttal in your mind as a person is speaking is a good way to increase your listening effectiveness.

5. ___T___   Our desire to talk before someone has finished speaking is the most common barrier to effective communication.

6. ___T___   Good listeners try to find useful information in any presentation or message.

7. ___F___   Having a negative reaction to a speaker's appearance will help you concentrate on their message.

8. ___T___   Active listening involves fully concentrating on what is being said and listening with all of your senses.

9. ___F___   It's a good practice to talk and listen at the same time.

10. ___T___   Identifying with the speaker means putting yourself in the speaker's place.

11. ___F___   When someone is speaking try to ask as many questions as possible.

12. ___T___   Try to focus all of your attention on the speaker.

13. ___F___   Uncontrolled emotions are a good way to increase your comprehension when listening to some speak.

14. ___T___   If you are using your mind and attention-span to formulate conclusions before the speaker is finished you may not hear the complete message.

15. ___F___   Do not pay attention to the body language of a speaker.

Power in Occupations

Application

Each of the following occupations comes with a certain amount of power. Why do you think the occupations have power?

Occupation	Reason for Having Power
Banker	*Example: Manages people's money*
Salesperson	
Artist	
Teacher	
Scientist	
Politician	
Lawyer	
Worker	
Engineer	
Minister	
Professional Athlete	
Journalist	
Entertainment celebrity	
Doctor	
Police Officer	
Army General	

Decision Making Worksheet
Mandatory Objectives
EXAMPLE

Decision to be made: _Location of new office building_

Mandatory Objectives

Alternatives	Close to town	Near public trans	4 offices	Large meeting room	Total Points
City center office	2	2	2	2	8
Vancouver Mall office	0	0	2	2	4
East side office	0	2	2	2	6

Decision Making

True or False Quiz

<u>**T or F**</u>

1. ___T___   Decision making is a responsibility.

2. ___T___   People, like your boss, will judge you on the quality of your decisions.

3. ___F___   Decisions do not involve judgments.

4. ___T___   Decisions involve making choices between alternative courses of action.

5. ___F___   You should never delegate routine decisions.

6. ___T___   Base your decisions on the best possible information.

7. ___F___   Impulsive decisions are always the best.

8. ___F___   When collecting information to use when making a decision, only collect that information which supports your personal viewpoint.

9. ___F___   Do not discuss your decisions with others.

10. ___F___   Decision making is becoming less important in the information age.

11. ___T___   The best kind of decision making process is objective and rational.

12. ___T___   The worst decision is no decision.

Problem Solving

Application

<u>Example Answers:</u>

1. Think of an organization in which you are an active member. This could be your school, church, business, etc. Write down the organization's name.

   Home Depot, Inc.

2. List some of the problems that you know have occurred in this organization during the past year.

   Understaffing

   Out of stock items

   Returned products

Remember, problems need not be negative actions -- any situation that called for collective thinking and finding a solution would qualify.

In the next section we will discuss a process for handling problems like the ones you listed above.

Conflict Management

Application

<u>Example Answers:</u>

Instructions:
Think of a conflict you have had in the recent past. This could be at school, work, or home.

1. Describe the conflict.

   I got into an argument with a coworker at the store. He said I had stock the shelves wrong.

2. How did you react?

   I got angry and yelled at him. Told him to mind his own business.

3. How did the other person or people react?

   He also got angry and told me to learn how to do my job.

4. What was the final outcome of this conflict?

   We both were angry and walked away upset.

5. Did it end on a positive or a negative note?

   Negative

6. Review the list of items that cause conflict. Was your conflict caused by one of these examples?

   I think it was caused by the other persons <u>desire for responsibility, authority, or control.</u>

7. List the underlying cause of your conflict.

   The other worker seemed to by trying to exert authority and control over me. They had the incorrect assumption that they were my superior because they had worked at the store longer.

26

Dealing with Conflict

Application

Example Answers:

1. List some of the positive methods you have used for dealing with conflict during the past few years.

   Talk things over with the other person.

   Tried not to place blame.

   Did not get angry at other person.

2. Which method do you consider to be the most positive? Explain why.

   Talking things over with the other person.

   This method seems to allow each person to make their point without getting upset.

Conflict Management
Application

<u>Suggestions:</u>
- After each pair of participants finishes their Plan of Action allow them to present their answers to the entire group.
- Facilitate a discussion about each plan and how well participants think it will work.
- If the conflict is real, steps 6 and 8 could be implemented.

Instructions: Work with a partner for this exercise.
Select a conflict situation. This can be a real conflict from your own experiences, or a fictional conflict --if the latter, make it realistic. Pretend that you have a conflict with your partner.

1. Describe your conflict situation.

2. Explore the causes of the conflict.

3. Negotiate a resolution to the conflict with the other person.

4. What steps should each person take in order to achieve a satisfactory resolution?

5. Write up a plan of action for your resolution.

6. Take Action.

7. If you are using a fictional conflict, discuss how well you think your resolution would really work.

8. If you are discussing a real conflict, try actually implementing your action plan and see if it really works - you might be surprised!

Prepared Public Speaking

Fill in the Blank Quiz

1. When selecting your speech topic it must be suited to the ___*audience*___, the occasion, and the allotted time.

2. A good speech must have a specific objective or ___*purpose*___.

3. A good title arouses ___*interest*___ and will make your listeners want to hear your speech.

4. When conducting research for your speech, read material that allows you to consider your topic from ___*all*___ ___*sides*___.

5. An outline will ensure that you present your thoughts in a coherent and ___*organized*___ manner.

6. The first part of your introduction should command the immediate ___*attention*___ of your audience.

7. The body of your speech has two main functions: to ___*explain*___ the subject and to ___*establish*___ the subject in the minds of your audience.

8. The conclusion of your speech should help the audience remember the ___*main*___ ___*points*___ of the speech.

9. The conclusion of your speech should include ___*repetition*___, ___*application*___, and ___*reinforcement*___.

10. Keeping an accurate list of sources will help you to complete a ___*bibliography*___.

11. When presenting a speech, proper ___*eye*___ ___*contact*___ is as essential as when you are engaged in a one on one conversation.

12. ___*Hand*___ ___*gestures*___ are important when delivering your speech but don't go overboard with them.

13. ___*Pacing*___ is also effective during your speech as long as you don't go overboard.

Team Mission Statement

Use this form to develop a mission statement. Answer questions one through three below. Next, write your own idea for a mission statement. When finished each member should present their answers and their mission statement to the group. The team should work together to bring each member's ideas together into a final mission statement.

Example Answers:

Team Name: *Anytown High School Associated Student Body*

1. What is the actual purpose of the team?
    Promote school spirit
    Decide on school activities
    Organize and conduct school activities
    Represent the interests of the student body

2. Who does the team serve?
    The student body of Anytown High School

3. How will the team work together to serve and to accomplish its purpose?
    Hold weekly ASB meetings
    Discuss activities and other school related matters
    Work as a team to conduct school activities

4. Draft mission statement.
    Anytown High School's ASB strives to unify students by planning school activities and encouraging student participation.

5. Final mission statement as agreed to by the members of the team.
    Anytown High School's ASB is a school-wide leadership group that strives to unify students positively and productively by planning school activities, encouraging student participation, and building school spirit making high school a positive experience for all.

Team Vision Statement

Use this form to develop a team vision statement. Write your own vision statement, then share it with your team. Combine ideas and create a perfect vision statement for your team.

Example Answers:

1. Team Name _____*Anytown High School ASB*_____

2. Vision Statement - Where the team would like to see itself or its organization in the future.

   The ASB team aims to achieve 100% student involvement in school activities by operating with class, positive energy, and integrity.

Team Goals

Use this form to develop team goals. Think of three goals for the coming year and record them on this form. Be sure the goals follow the SMART goal guidelines. When each member is finished, share your goals with the team. The team will need to combine goals and agree on which goals to adopt for the year, or other time frame as needed.

Example Answers:

Team Name_____*Anytown High School ASB*_____

Goal 1

Organize a school spirit assembly to kick off the new school year.

Goal 2

Organize a Holiday dance during December.

Goal 3

_____

_____

_____

Goal 4

_____

_____

_____

Parliamentary Procedure Terms
Matching Quiz

1. Assembly __L__   A. To agree with the chair

2. Business at hand __R__   B. Officer or person in charge of conducting a meeting

3. Chairperson __B__   C. Small group with a specific job

4. Consideration __O__   D. To be relevant to then motion

5. Commit __J__   E. To be on the winning side

6. Committee __C__   F. To finish speaking and sit down

7. Delegate __S__   G. Do this before you speak

8. Have the Floor __M__   H. Must happen before a motion can be discussed

9. Germane __D__   I. Normally the president

10. Maker of the motion __T__   J. Refer to a committee

11. Nominations __Q__   K. Current motion before the group

12. Pending __K__   L. All the members

13. Presiding officer __I__   M. To be recognized and have the right to speak

14. Prevailing __E__   N. Formal approval

15. Question __P__   O. To discuss an item or motion

16. Ratify __N__   p. Are you ready to vote?

17. Second __H__   Q. Happens before the election of new officers

18. Sustain __A__   R. The current business

19. Recognized __G__   S. Give someone a task

20. Yield the floor __F__   T. The one who makes the motion

Parliamentary Procedure

Review Questions

Write in the correct term or phrase

1. The phrase referring to the order in which business should be dealt with in a meeting.
   Order of business

2. Sets expectations for a meeting and helps keep everyone at the meeting on track so time is not wasted.
   Agenda

3. The official record of the proceedings of a meeting .
   Minutes

4. The chairperson uses this object to signal the passage or failure of any motions.
   Gavel

5. The customary method of voting on a motion by saying "aye" or "no."
   Voice vote

6. Called for when the presiding officer, or a member, has doubts about a previous vote.
   Rising vote

7. Means that half or more of the members present must vote in favor of a motion for it to pass. For example, if 100 members were present 51 would have to vote in favor to pass.
   Majority vote

8. Needed when a motion will limit the rights of a member or members of the organization.
   Two thirds vote

9. The number of vote-entitled members who must be present in order for business to be legally transacted.
   Quorum

10. Used by any individual at the meeting to bring forward their idea or proposal for adoption by the group.
    Main motion

11. Used to modify or change a main motion.
    Amend

Communication

Review Questions

1. There are many forms of communication in today's world. Why doesn't this guarantee good communication?
    Sometimes people don't have good communication skills.

2. What is the basic purpose of communication?
    Exchange of information.

3. What is necessary for communication to be effective?
    Sender and receive must both be good communicators.

4. List the three primary purposes of communication.
    To inform, influence, express feelings.

5. List the 9 key components of the communication process.
    Time, place, situation, sender, receiver, message, channel, feedback, interference.

6. What does it mean to say that the sender must encode the message?
    Put it in a form the receiving person will understand.

7. What does it mean to say that the receiver must decode the message?
    Changed into a form the receiver can understand.

8. What is feedback and why is it so important?
    The way the receiver responds to a message. Tells the sender if the message was received properly.

9. What is interference and how does it affect the communication process?
    Anything that blocks the message from actually reaching the receiver. Can interrupt the communication process.

Verbal Communication

Matching Quiz

1. __H__   Be Accurate and Know Your Topic

2. __A__   Consider Your Listener

3. __O__   Speak Clearly

4. __M__   Speak at a Moderate Pace

5. __B__   Select Words Carefully

6. __E__   Use the Active Voice

7. __J__   Be Courteous

8. __L__   Be Your Natural Self

9. __G__   Have Empathy for the Other Person

10. __I__   Be Concise

11. __N__   Don't Talk Too Much

12. __D__   Listen Intently

13. __P__   Don't Talk Over the Other Person

14. __K__   Maintain Proper Eye Contact

15. __C__   Use Proper Tone

16. __F__   Tailor Your Message to the Person or Audience You are Speaking to

Body Language

True or False Quiz

<u>**T or F**</u>

1. ___F___   A person with their arms crossed during a conversation can indicate that they agree with the opinions or actions of other individuals with whom they are communicating.

2. ___T___   Nail biting can demonstrate stress, nervousness, or insecurity.

3. ___T___   A hand placed on the cheek can indicate that a person is lost in thought, or is considering something.

4. ___F___   Tapping or drumming the fingers demonstrates that a person is patient and does not mind waiting.

5. ___T___   Head tilted to one side can demonstrate that a person is listening keenly, or is interested in what is being communicated.

6. ___F___   Touching the nose can demonstrate that an individual is being truthful about what they are saying.

7. ___T___   Rubbing the hands together might mean an individual is excited for something or is waiting in anticipation

8. ___T___   Placing the tips of the fingers together can be a demonstration of control and authority.

9. ___F___   Palms open, facing upwards can be a sign of dishonesty.

10. ___T___   Head in hands can demonstrate boredom, or it might show that a person is upset or ashamed and does not want to show their face.

11. __F__   Locked ankles can communicate calmness.

12. __T__   Standing up straight with shoulders back, often shows that a person is feeling confident.

13. __T__   Stroking of the beard or chin can communicate deep thought.

14. __F__   Pulling the ear can often mean the person is having a easy time coming to a conclusion in their thinking when they are trying to make a decision.

15. __F__   Avoiding eye contact usually indicates confidence and an extroverted personality.

16. __T__   Lips held tightly together can mean the person is angry or very serious about something.

17. __F__   Eye brows raised up shows the person is bored or is very defensive.

18. __T__   Sitting on the edge of your chair can create the impression that you are "on the edge" and nervous.

Telephone Skills
Fill in the Blank Quiz

1. When answering the telephone for a business try to answer on the __*first*__ ring.

2. When greeting a customer on the phone be sure to __*identify*__ yourself.

3. If a caller does not want to be placed on hold, offer to *return the call* .

4. When you return to a caller who has been placed on hold, you should first get their attention by stating __*their*__ __*name*__ .

5. If a caller resists being transferred to another person in your organization, offer to take their __*number*__ so the right person can call them back.

6. You should let the __*caller*__ hang up first when ending a phone call.

7. If someone calls for a co-worker who is out of the office you should offer to take a __*message*__ .

8. When taking a message you should include the __*action*__ to be taken.

9. If you have a second call coming in while you are on the phone with a customer, you can put the first caller on hold, but be sure to return to them __*promptly*__ .

10. Screening calls involves getting the caller's __*name*__ in a courteous and professional manner.

11. When making a call you should __*identify*__ yourself.

12. You should try to project a good telephone __*image*__ .

13. Avoid __*slang*__ expressions.

14. Always project a sincere __*interest*__ in the caller.

39

15. A _moderate_ rate and tone of voice is best.

16. When dealing with an angry caller keep your voice _calm_.

17. Don't _contradict_ an angry caller.

18. Discuss _solutions_ that will help solve the caller's problem.

19. If an angry caller continues to use profanity on the phone it is okay to _hang_ _up_.

Texting
True or False Quiz

1.   __F__   Responding to a text within three days is usually considered appropriate.

2.   __F__   Longer texts are better than short ones.

3.   __T__   Don't call in response to a text without asking.

4.   __T__   Don't get impatient if someone doesn't respond right away.

5.   __F__   Sarcasm in a text message is a great way to communicate with people you don't know very well.

6.   __F__   People are never offended by sarcasm.

7.   __T__   Double-check your autocorrect.

8.   __T__   Double check who you're sending it to.

9.   __F__   If you are late for a date or other appointment, don't text the person to let them know. They will figure it out.

10.   __T__   Don't text while driving.

11.   __T__   Make sure you know the correct meaning of abbreviations before using them.

12.   __F__   Use any texting laughter abbreviations you want to make up.

13.   __F__   Using all caps is a great way to text.

14.   __F__   Texting while you are out with other people is always a good idea.

15.   __T__   You could get hurt if you text while you are walking.

16.   __T__   Communicate clearly and text exactly what you mean to say.

www.ingramcontent.com/pod-product-compliance
Lightning Source LLC
Chambersburg PA
CBHW081645220526
45468CB00009B/2558